RELEASE THE GREATNESS THAT'S WITHIN YOU
Including Fears, Forces, & Antidotes

by Barbara A. Perry

GARDEN 33 PUBLISHER
P. O. BOX 197
Aiken, S.C. 29802

Release The Greatness That's Within You
Barbara A. Perry

Copyright © 2014 by Barbara A. Perry

All Rights Reserved.

ISBN: 978-0-9960442-0-2

Unless otherwise noted, Scriptures quotations are from the King James Version of the Bible.
Copyright © 1989 Thomas Nelson, Inc., publishers.

NO PART OF THIS BOOK MAY BE REPRODUCED IN ANY FORM, BY PHOTOCOPING OR BY ANY ELECTRONIC OR MECHANICAL MEANS, INCLUDING INFORMATION STORAGE OR RETRIEVAL SYSTEMS, WITHOUT PERMISSION IN WRITING FROM THE COPYRIGHT OWNER/AUTHOR.

Printed in the U.S.A.

GARDEN 33 PUBLISHER
P. O. Box 197
Aiken, S.C. 29802

To

The Glory and Honor of

Almighty God

CONTENTS

		Page
	Introduction...	6
	Why I Must Try..	7
1	Reach Higher..	8
2	Shackled	15
3	More Than A Conqueror	18
4	Presumed Dead	24
5	The Steel Door..	28
6	Peoples	33
7	Awake Oh My Soul!................................	35
8	Fears, Forces, and Antidotes.................	36

Introduction

I believe greatness lies within each human being. As we live a spirit filled life in Christ, we can flourish in greatness and enjoy our wealthy place in Him. Jesus said, **"He came to give us life abundantly." John 10:10** I believe it. So I must try to reach you through my writings in hopes that you will come to see and accept that you can rise up from where you are and live out your hopes and dreams. The dream of not just being a model for others to follow, but also to aid in helping others to become models.

Preface

WHY I MUST TRY

Why I Must Try…

Why I must try when the odds seem against me? I must try because the odds are not to prevent me but to construct the inner me. The odds are to squeeze the greatness out of me.

Why I Must Try…

Why I must try when I am rejected? I must try because rejection is an ignorance part of humans who don't know or care to know the greatness of what I have to offer or what I can accomplish.

Why I Must Try…

I must try for my children, your children and those to follow. I must try for you, for me, for the one life or for the many lives that could be touch. Not tallying the ones that I did, but keeping the dream alive by the ones I could.

Why I Must Try…

I must try for the destitute, the inferior, the inadequate, the inefficient, the lacking, the under nourish, the needy, the penniless, and the broken. I must try for the effort that what I have started others will join in.

REACH HIGHER

What do I have that will possible make a different? What do I have that can help you along life's journey? What do I have to share that will stir the greatness in you? I have good news! Good news that you can become, do and perform. There is an innate ability within you waiting to be developed. It can be developed through life in Christ. There's a dream, a vision within you that's waiting to be born. You can give birth to it through life in Christ. You can defeat the odds! You can bring forth, you can do and perform by living life in Christ. The Lord said,**" Remain in me, and I will remain in you. No branch can bear fruit by itself; it must remain in the vine. Neither can you bear fruit unless you remain in me. I am the vine; you are the branches. If a man remains in me and I in him, he will bear much fruit; apart from me you can do nothing." John 15:4,5**

When I was young, I wanted to teach, model and write a book, but somewhere along life's journey those interests fell asleep. I tried to write a book once, but it was a great challenge - so it was never completed. I was interviewed for a teacher's aid, but I just didn't cut it. I dressed up to attend a show for potential models - but my ride didn't show up.

Well, I got married, went to college, got a certificate and went to work in the legal field. I later received Christ and those desires were revived. I learned that they were more than just desires; they were dreams, abilities and gifts that were deposited within me by God. Dreams and abilities God would use to cause me to see that without Him I could do nothing. The dream without him would never become a reality. It will just remain a dream without abilities (power). But with him the dream will come true, for He will make me to be productive. With Him the dream would have a foundation with structure.

The Lord wasn't slow in starting His work in me. The first writing that he used in developing the inner me was *"From A Seed To A Tree"*. God used this writing to plant and grow up the church that was started as a result of my salvation and call to the ministry. As I remained in the LORD and studied His Word, I begin to bear fruit (increase). I remember God telling me that I will write what He wanted me to write.

The 1st writing *"From A Seed To A Tree"* included essentials that spiritually educated us on what was needful in growing strong in the Lord. The required essential: (a) A New Spirit (b) Read, Memorize and Meditate (c) Trust In God (d) Expect (e) Prayer (f) Fasting & Prayer (g) Giving (h) Remain in God.

Other writings followed; such as, *"Fear, Forces, and Antidotes"*. *Fear, Forces, and Antidotes* taught us about certain fears that can hold us in bondage, the forces that are behind the fears and the antidotes the Lord have provided for our freedom. Titles include: The Fear of the Unknown, The Fear of People, Rejection and Phobias.

"The Robe of The One Who Cares" is a booklet that displays Jesus as your covering for shame - past, present and future.

These writings were not only used within the local church, but were given in booklet form as seed to others. Free copies were left in Christian bookstores, convenient stores and in laundry mats.

Truly, apart from Him I can do nothing. I could not have written these writings without Him. It was a big struggle and a challenge to try it without Him, but with Him, He removed the struggle of what to write and how to write it.

I would not use my weak writing skills and grammar as an excuse not to try. I believe God wouldn't allow the lack of grammar or writing skills prevent His Good News from blessing you. I would not lift up a Moses' excuse before God. I peeked at my lack of ability, but I looked at God's ability. I wanted it and He wanted to perform it in and through me. I said, yes! I would not reject the ministry God prepared for me! The ministry is my purpose for fulfilling my love to God and to you. It is the avenue in which God uses to be a blessing to you. (For I will bless you and make you a blessing." **Gen. 12:2**)

Rejection of ministry is rebellion against God!

Through Jesus, the dream and the desire are coming true. The reality of it is taking true form. Jesus is making me to be that Teacher, Author & Model. I am becoming. To become is power! Greatness is surfacing! When I speak of greatness, I'm not relating it to fame or money.

Greatness is the power/ability to do and perform in spite of the odds. Greatness is to shine on the inside and cast a reflection on the outside. Whatever is shining on the inside of you should be coming out in some way, form or fashion. Your God given abilities should be put to use, not hidden. Greatness is part of you being a new creation in Christ. If you didn't have it before, you got it now! Greatness comes through Christ. Christ is your greatness and He lives within you.

"Greater is He that is in you than he that is in the world." I John 4:4 Greatness comes along with the new creation, but it has to be developed. It's part of your spiritual inheritance as a child of the King.

Don't be content to stay at one level of greatness; seek maximization so you can do greater works. Seek to excel in the dream that was endowed upon you. Invest in your dream; no matter how small the portion is make use of it. A little can become a lot, if handled wisely. Don't despise the day of small beginnings.

When developing in greatness, fear, shame and embarrassment can be obstacles; but you must step out of them. Greatness diminishes fear and allows you to have good success. It replaces fear with courage and confidence in one's ability to do, perform and carry out.

As greatness begins to surface, you perceive a clearer vision of your purpose and its fulfillment.

God has a Plan and a Purpose for your life and you have a Goal.

Purpose

The greatest purpose for your life and mine is to Love the Lord our God and to seek the betterment of our life and the life of others (to love our neighbor as our self). It is written, **"Teacher, which is the greatest commandment in the Law? Jesus replied: 'Love the Lord your God with all your heart and with all your soul and with all your mind.' This is the first and greatest commandment. And the second is like it: 'Love your neighbor as yourself.' All the Law and the Prophets hang on these two commandments." Matt. 22:36-40**

Plan

God's plan: God has a plan for you to fulfill purpose. Jesus' death, burial and resurrection are God's plan for fulfilling purpose on his end. God first loved us. Now he says to love Him and man. Through salvation and life in Christ Jesus, we fulfill purpose on our end. As you follow through with purpose: guidance, direction, and perception on God's plan for your individual life will be made known. You will be given knowledge on what you are to do or become. The Lord will guide you on the right avenue in carrying out purpose.

Goal

Our goal in God's plan in carrying out and fulfilling purpose is to press through with faith, courage, perseverance/persistence and determination. Trust God that He called you to this and He will equip you with what you need to perform it. **"Jesus is the Author and Finisher of our faith." Hebrews 12:2**

Growing in greatness and fulfilling purpose summarized:

    1) Without Christ and faith in Him we can do nothing.
    2) Prayer and diligent study in the Word.
    3) Greatness is developed. Power/ability comes.
    4) Perception/clearer view of purpose and plan.

SHACKLED

You Don't Have to Remain Shackled!

shackle – 1. a metal fastening, usu. one of a pair, for encircling and confining the ankle or wrist of a prisoner or captive; fetter; manacle. 2. often shackles. Something that confines or restrains.

Has something in the past or present happened in your life or someone else life that placed metal fastener on your being? Are you shackled down in your heart and you are not free to rise? Whatever it is, it's keeping you shackled. Shackled in a prison of bitterness, unforgiveness, hatefulness, vengeful, etc. These are shackles of sin. These sins are affecting you in spirit, mind, will and emotions. They are ultimate keeping you from developing and reaching greatness and achieving you purpose and goal in life. Unless these shackled are broken off, you will be held back. You're like a tree trunk without branches or vines. You have roots but sin has shut off your source of life. You can't prosper nor produce, nor perform. You don't have any power to reproduce, multiply nor bring forth increase in the inner man (the seat of greatness). Your being have become like pieces of scattered puzzle. You can't see the whole picture until the pieces of the puzzle is put together. When sin is removed, the picture in the puzzle is seen in color.

You don't have to remain shackled in sin. You can choose today to be free. Choose wisely: Bondage in sin or greatness in life with freedom. You may find it difficult or impossible for the shackles to be removed, but in Christ Jesus you can be free from the shackles of sin, today! If you so desire to be free and regain life, pray the prayer at the end of the following page.

Unforgiveness & forgiveness

Forgiveness brings healing from hurtfulness. You may have experienced a lot of hurtful and painful things in life, but you have to forgive those that wronged you for your own health and wholeness' sake. Unforgiveness brings in sickness.

Unforgiveness doesn't just cause you to suffer but someone else in your life is being affected by it. Is it your child? A loved one? A friend? A relationship? Why hold them in bondage with you? Let go of it! Be refreshed and recapture your dream for them and for you!

When seeking to excel in life, you want to move from one level to another. Unforgiveness and other sins hold you back from reaching that higher level of excellence. When you harbor sin in your heart, you will never know how high you can fly or how much you can blossom in your calling, gift, talent or ability in life. Christ came to give you an abundant life now and in the end to come everlasting life. He desires above all things that you prosper in your life on earth. For in this He takes joy in! **III John 2**

If you want to receive Jesus as your Lord and Savior pray this Salvation Prayer: *Lord Jesus, be merciful to me a sinner and save my soul. I admit that I am a sinner. Today Lord, I repent of my sins and ask you to come into my heart. I believe you are the Son of the living God and that you died and rose again. Lord Jesus, give me of your Spirit that I may live this new life in you. Help me to let go of this sin of _____ that I have harbor in mine heart. Create within me a clean heart and renew a right spirit within me. Thank You, Jesus! Amen.*

MORE THAN A CONQUEROR

You may be down but you don't have to stay down. You may be depressed about life or in a pit of some sort: you can surface to the top. Self-pity may have a hold on you but you can stop being the tail and become the head. Get to know who you are on the inside. Take time to examine where you came from. Stop looking so hard on the outside; you'll only perceive darkness. Probe into the Bible, you'll perceive hopefulness. The Bible is a shining light filled with truth.

Spend time with your Creator. You can learn a lot about the ability within you, when you get to know the stock you're cut from: the image you're created in. You can ever accept some things about yourself and rise up. You have created power within you. When you were created, you were crowned with glory and honor. The same Mighty God that created the universe is the same mighty spirit that lives within you. When God breathe the breath of life in you, there was more to that breath than oxygen. God's organism also flowed in you.

Yes! A living, active spirit was deposited in you: A spirit of might and power.

Believe in yourself! God believes in you! He has every reason to; because He knows whose image you are created in.

God can take your little bit of ability and turn it into supernatural ability. Read **Judges 6:11- 40; 7 & 8 c**hapter. When Gideon was saying negative things about himself, God was speaking great things about him. When Gideon thought he couldn't defeat the enemy, God said, " I'm going to be with you." When God is on your side, you can rise up! You can become more than a conqueror!

Stop comparing yourself to others. We're not to compare our self to others. God is one of a kind. God made you one of a kind. We all have various personality and differences. Every snowflake is shaped different. No two is alike. God made them that way for a reason: Consider. Every person has a different fingerprint: Think about it. We're not to compare our self to others. We're not to try to be them. When we do, we reject the image we are created in. When we do, we position our self to lose our identity and our potential. If you weren't born a twin, stop trying to be one and if you don't have a twin don't try to make one. It's a heavy load trying to be like someone else. By the way, that person is only flesh and flesh decays and dies.

Why waste years trying to be like someone else, and at the end of your years you never knew whom you were. Who will give an answer as to the person you were? Don't say it doesn't matter because it does. It matters to your children, grandchildren, etc. They use it to measure if they came from a family of honor or dishonor. It helps them to relate and identify themselves. It helps them to understand many things about themselves. If you don't like yourself very well, then you don't know much about yourself. You don't need anyone to degrade you, cause you are doing a pretty good job of it yourself. We can find hundreds of reasons not to like our self, but how offer do we seek reasons to like our self. We are our own worst enemy. We notice that we are lacking in certain abilities within our self; immediately we criticize our self. If we are going to be our own critic, let it be for improvement not for quitting. We should rather seek God's opinion of our shortfalls and seek ways to improve. There are things that I fell short in, but the Lord taught me how to profit where I could become the head and not the tail, above and not beneath. I followed his instructions and He rewarded me. I could have languished in self-pity and depression – but I didn't – I was willing to find out what was in store for me. I have a dream, a future and a hope. I'm going further! I'm pursuing what God has for me. I have plans to return to college and pursue a degree in the arts, and if it is in line with God's plan, then no devil in hell is going to steal it from me. Yes! I have a future and a hope. What about you? There were some hard things thrown in my path; but through God's grace, He strengthen me to press through them. He opened up heaven's treasure to me and I received! He will do the same for you!

You are a piece of gold, but you're never know how you can sparkle until you stop trying to copy someone's else physique and allow Christ to refine you. You are a beautiful person: a rare gem waiting to be discovered. Christ will show you how special you are and why he gave you different attribute from others.

Make a commitment to yourself that for a month, you are going to stop comparing yourself to others and just seek out the treasures within you. Ask Christ to supervise you in this venture of getting to know the person, liking the person, and accepting the person He made in His image. Talk to Him about yourself. Ask Him questions about yourself. Allow Him to counsel you on learning to accept and like yourself. Take notes!

The devil, your enemy, seeks to cut you down to nothing. He will have you seeing darkness when the sun is shining in high noon. Every negative statement you quote about yourself, the devil strengthen the power to that statement. He uses those negative statements to transform your mind into his. Stop allowing the devil to control you thinking. He is a horrible influence. He uses negative statements to shape your present and future. Those negative statements are like bricks you are laying down to make a path. Each step on the path leads you deeper into deception about yourself. You keep opening doors of pessimism for your tomorrow; each day you rise, you walk through another door of gloom and despair. Your mind is in prison to deception. You have agreed with the devil that you are what he says you are. **Jesus said, "The devil is a liar and the father of lies."** You have believed lies far too long. It is time for the Truth. You need a change and you need it now! You need to rise up out of that stink bed of lies and take a bath! You need to soak yourself in the Word of God and be transformed by the renewing of your mind by the Truth!

The devil is an instigator in the weapons he uses to deceive. One of his major weapons that he uses in tearing down a person is – the spirit of comparison. He uses it to influence you to believe that you are less than who you are.

When you seek to be like someone other than Christ, then you become less than rather than greater than. Comparison can make you feel so tiny, when you come in the presence of someone more educated or knowledgeable than you. You can allow that spirit of comparison to become imprinted in your mind to the point where you feel like a grasshopper or a no body. You need to get rid of that grasshopper mentality and take hold of your inheritance in Christ in being more than a conqueror. Good things can happen to you and through you, when you align yourself with what God is doing and accepts that He wants to do it through you. God wants to crown you with glory and honor. Allow him to use you to effectuate change in the world and touch a life!

PRESUMED DEAD

presume – 3 : to suppose to be true without proof 2 : to expect or assume esp. with confidence

So no one knows that you exist. Maybe they don't know, but that's no excuse to stop living, dreaming, planning, or pursuing. When Moses fled Egypt, he dwelled in Midian. After a period of time, his loved ones and his enemies presumed him to be dead. They imagined he was lost at sea or drowned while crossing the Red Sea. Most likely many of them thought he died while walking in the desert heat, by a snake bite, a scorpion sting, or devour by a wild beast. They were feeling sadness and grief for him, but Moses had embraced a new beginning in life. He started a new occupation, got married, and had children. He had found contentment.

The Moses that left Egypt wasn't the same Moses that returned to Egypt. He left Egypt a murder in fear of his life, but returned to Egypt a man of God with power, a Deliverer, and a Prophet. He spent 40 years on the backside of a desert, but it was the right side: next door to God. After Moses left Egypt, God revealed himself as his neighbor. Yes, when he left Egypt he moved closer to God and God to him. For 40 years something amazing was happening within him that was unknown by others – 40 years of being transformed before being revealed. It took forty years, but He was right where God needed him to be to prepare him for great works.

When Moses fled Egypt, he was unknowingly traveling in the right direction, because God was divinely guiding him (He knew the plan he had for Moses, just as he knows the plan he has for you). God was looking out of Heaven's window watching Moses development over the years while he waited for the right time to reveal Himself to him.

God's plan involved him investing 40 years of teaching and training into Moses' life while shaping him to be a leader to shepherd His flock.

When aspiring to new heights, there are investments that have to be made to shape you, to get you ready, to make you more productive for what you're reaching for. Some places of shaping aren't always pleasant. The unpleasant places are where your investments yield rewards. Investing time, patience, discipline, and even courage builds internal tenacity and fortitude. The unpleasant places are the places where the soil is turned upside down, inside out, twirled around, and interwoven to produce a better texture to give you a favorable chance of being chosen by the right person or company. They most likely went through the same process that you're going through.

God was watching Moses coming and going while he was in Egypt and in Midian. He wasn't just watching him, but developing him. Moses was unaware that a life changing encounter awaited him. A life changing encounter is waiting for you, if you don't give up. It may not be Moses' burning bush encounter, but it will be an encounter that will usher you into his glory and/or your dream, destiny, or vision.

God grants favor and open doors of opportunities. He schedules divine meetings. He places the right people/person in your path or causes thing to turn in your favor. Have faith in God. If there seems to be no way, trust him to create a way. Don't give up hope, but turn loose your faith and watch our Almighty God do the impossible in your life, circumstance, situation, or condition.

You may not become well known, but stick with God and he

will keep you off his presume dead list. And remember, aged wine is fine wine. It takes time, even years before it is introduced to the public.

THE STEEL DOOR: WHAT IS AGAINST YOU?

³¹ What shall we say to these things? If God be for us, who can be against us? ³² He that spared not his own Son, but delivered him up for us all, how shall he not with him also freely give us all things?" Rom. 8:31,32

In December 2012 I dream of walking down the sidewalk of a building to pick up my paycheck. When I came to the door (the door was made out of steel). I discovered that it could not be open from the outside, but only from the inside. There was another person standing some feet away. As soon as I discover the condition of the steel door, my thought was, "I couldn't get in." But then it supernaturally opened. It was bright on the inside and a group of people were standing around the front of a counter waiting for their checks. I was standing in the back. The person who was issuing the checks looked up and saw me. She started flipping through the piles of checks to find mine. Standing in the back, I supernaturally saw it before she did. She found it, pulled it out, reach over the groups of people and handed it to me. The people arrived before me, were in line before me, but I got mine before them. (God preferred favor). I didn't have to tell her mine name, she already knew it as if she was familiar with me. When I left out the building, I looked at my check. It was more than I expected. I rejoiced, and went on my way.

My dream is to become a best seller author while still ministering God's word to the Church. In the natural world this dream is like a steel door that can only be opened from the inside. I'm standing on the outside looking at the steel door (I'm facing stiff competition, I have no influence, no one knows me, and no money). But I'm still writing in faith that God will cause it to happen. I completed one of my three books. After a while, I took up the task of writing query letters and proposals. I sent them in to various agents, but they were rejected. Rejected does not feel good, but by the grace and strength of God it wasn't enough to stop me. There are no dead ends with God only supernatural openings.

We have to use rejection constructively. When you are rejected, see it as "that's not the one, that's not the way, etc." When my query letters or proposals are rejected by an agent or publisher, it is because that is not the one God has in place for me.

One evening that steel door thought hit me. The weight of the impossibility of it caused me to cry. This may sound strange to some – in the natural I was crying, I felt cast down, but yet my inner spirit was strong and I was releasing faith to God to still make it possible. I needed to release the pressure of it. I needed to cry out all the things that were against me. I was under spiritual attack from the enemy. I was also crying about the reality of it happening to me. In my spirit I could see it happening. I was experiencing the desire of it happening. After a little while, I got alright. My composure was restored and I was back at working on the proposals. I was being plowed, but courage, determination, and tenacity pulled me out. The manifestation of a fortified spirit surfaced. The Holy Spirit strengthened my inner person.

If you truly want your dream to come true, you have to work hard. If your dream is alive in you, it's going to be like a birth, a baby pushing to come out. You can allow the labor pains to kill the dream or give birth to it. There will be labor pains. There is no way around them: breathe softly on the onset of contractions; they will pass.

One evening, I was sitting at the dinner table eating and thinking about getting my books published. The steel door thought came to me again. But this time it didn't weaken me. The Lord dropped Romans 8:31 in my spirit, *"If God be for us, who can be against us?"* That was a strong message from the LORD. He also gave me this message, "With Him there is always room for one more." No matter how big those giants of influence, competition, or unknown may be, there is always room for one more with Him. You may seem small and unimportant before steel doors, but when you have the favor of God on the other side no steel door is going to keep you out! You and I have to take heart (be encouraged) that God is for us. His plan is to will direct our pathway when we yield all our ways unto him. You may have done it this way and that way, but it just didn't work. You may have done a 90° turn and it still didn't work. Well good! Now, do an about face and let God lead/show you His way. He said he will instruct us and teach us in the way we should go. He will watch over us and counsel us.

The Lord has something good he wants to give you, but don't expect it to be serve on a silver platter. He wants to give you your own land flowing with milk and honey — just keep holding on to his hand. Start reaching for what God have for you. God will assign an Overseer (Angel) to aid you in reaching your destiny, your mission, greater prosperity, etc. You stay with him and He will stay with you and bring you into that wealthy place or Garden of Eden.

PEOPLES

Along the road to greatness, you will encounter various peoples. Some will be for you and some will be against you. Some will work to help you, but some will work to hinder you. You must face them with courage. They will seek to put fear in you and say things to discourage you, but you must meet them boldly. Be wise and courageous enough to step out from their zones. You will encounter people who are afraid of who you are, what you can do and what you can become. If you become, you can make a different. **To become is power!** There are people in every class that fears power. So they seek to keep you in slavery or subordinate to them. Everything is okay with you and them until you start talking about becoming. When you start to rise up to become, negative attitudes from others are going to rise up also. At that point you are going to have to make a decision: bondage to people or freedom to greatness. Don't be quit to give yourself away to people. A smile is just a greeting – move in cautiously. You heard it once, you heard it twice, now you will hear it again: Smiling Faces Tells Lies! If you converse with some folk long enough, you will find that their heart is not with you.

You be a trustworthy person, but don't be so trusting when it comes to people. Jesus did not give himself away to people for he knew what was in man's heart. [John 2:24,25]   If you're not careful, people can drain and rob you of your dreams: if you allow them to. Apply wisdom as you examine the situation.   One class of people is not superior over another. One class is not more intelligent than the other. It's what you do with what you got! We all have weaknesses and strengths. One person may be strong in one area but weak in another area and vice versa. We all have a brain. We all have a heart. We all have a mouth. Seek wisdom. Seek knowledge and get understanding; it will keep you safe and prosper you along life's way!

CONCLUSION

AWAKE OH MY SOUL!

Awake, oh my soul and arise to the call! Sleep no longer, but arise! Possess your inheritance! Reach out oh my soul and by wisdom take hold of what is rightly your! Oh my soul, sit not as a beggar! Oh my soul, be strengthen with might! Rise up and overcome! Take spear and sword and strike! Wake up, rise up and run through a troop! Be empowered my soul and leap over this wall! My soul, be gird with God's strength for he makes your way to be complete! My soul, your feet are like the feet of a deer! You tread over the roughest of the enemy territory without fear; with each step your feet is made sure! My soul, by the power of God rise up and pursue your enemies until they be overtaken! My soul, rest not in the bonds of slumber! Do not find rest until all thy enemies have been consumed!

Let it be Lord Jesus, let it be!

FEARS, FORCES, & ANTIDOTES

<u>Preface</u>

As humans we all have a specific fear or some specific fears that we need to conquer. There are many kinds of fears, but I will only teach on 4 of them (The Fear of the Unknown, The Fear of People, The Fear of Rejection, and Phobias).

Whatever kind of fear has taken hold of you, there is a way to conquer over it. In this teaching, I will talk about the fear, the force behind the fear, and share with you a scripture antidote to conquer that fear.

I will now share with you 5 bondages that fear causes:

- Fear causes failure
- Fear locks doors
- Fear paralyzes (render you powerless)
- Fear suffocates
- Fear makes cowards

Fear No. 1
The Fear of the Unknown

The unknown can be the next hour, next day, the next month, the next year or your future.

Many folks fear what will happen from hour to hour or day to day. They fear what will happen as they leave the house, get in the car, ride a bus, etc. They fear what is waiting around the corner for them as they go about their daily activities. Many fear what will be ahead for them if they are suddenly without the use of a car, if they lose their job, their spouse or someone or something they hold dear.

The Force:
Self-ability, self-dependent, and a dis-trustful heart in the Creator. A dis-connected
relationship with the Creator.

The all-wise, eternal, immoral, invincible, ever present God, knows what happened in your life yesterday; He knows what's happening in your life right now, and He knows what will happen in our life tomorrow and forever.

For the eyes of the Lord run to and fro throughout the whole earth,... II Chronicles 16:9

"Neither is there any creature that is not manifest in (hidden from) his sight: but all things are naked and opened unto the eyes of him with whom we have to do (must give account)." Hebrews 4:13

The Antidote:
Trust and dependence in God is the key factor for overcoming this fear.

God is your creator. He desires to be a part of your life, and calm your fear of the unknown.

When you place your trust in Him, you will not fear that your next move will end in disaster, failure, despair, or death. He knows your past. He holds your present and future in His hands.

Whatever calamities or troubles you may face in the next hour, day, month or year, you don't have to face them alone or in fear. The Lord says, *" I will never leave you nor forsake you."* Heb. 13:5

God already know your unknown. God is already ahead of you. Deut. 31:8 states, *"And the LORD is the one who goes ahead of you; He will be with you. He will not fail you nor forsake you. Do not fear, or be dismayed (don't faint, don't lose heart and don't lose courage)."*

Trust your unknown into the hands of God-Creator of time and eternity. When you fear the unknown, it opens the doors to anxiety and worry, but when you place your trust in the Lord, you will be at peace. *"Thou wilt keep him in perfect peace, whose mind is stayed on thee: because he trusteth in thee."* Isaiah 26:3

You will have courage to declare, *" I will not fear, though the earth should change, and though the mountains slip into the heart of the sea, though its waters roar and foam, though the mountains quake at its swelling pride* [comes from Psalm 46:2,3]*."*

Additional Scriptures Reading for Fear of the Unknown:

Matthew 6:24-34
Matthew 10: 26-31
I Peter 1:3-5
I Peter 5:7
Isaiah 35
Isaiah 60
Jeremiah 29: 10-14
Revelation 21: 1-8

Fear No. 2
The Fear of People

There are many reasons why we fear others: their status, their title, the position they hold, more knowledgeable, their color, their wealth, etc.

The Force:
Insecurity or lacking self-confidence

People have a tendency of comparison. When comparison is set in motion, it highlights our lack, weakness, or inability. These shiny off-sets produces fear in one person and causes the other person to appear as a great one to be highly esteemed. Before them we calculate our own life and position and the value = low self-esteem (a nobody).

We have a tendency of viewing others from the position that we are in. We compare one aspect to another; our education, I.Q., background, speech, prosperity, failures, success, etc. And from that position of view, the other person is as a god on earth.

The Antidote:

1ˢᵗ. Fear God (Compare man to God)
2ⁿᵈ. Find out who image all people were created in.

In Matt. 10:28 it is written, *"And fear not them which kill the body, but are not able to kill the soul: but rather fear him which is able to destroy both soul and body in hell."*

Let your fear be in God Almighty-Creator. Your fear should not be in what man can do, but in what God can do. We are to submit ourselves to one another in humbleness: not fearful or cowardly.

"Submitting yourselves one to another in the fear of God." Ephesians 5:21

"Let nothing be done through strife or vain glory; <u>but in lowliness of mine let each esteem other better than themselves.</u>" Philippians 2:3

If you have a real problem on overcoming this fear, join me in prayer: Lord, I confess that fear is a major obstacle that I need to defeat. I ask for help in this area. Help me to overcome this fear and stand with courage and humbleness of mind. Amen.

God created man from the dust of the ground (Genesis 2:7) and then He revealed what flesh is in Isaiah 40: 6,7,8 and it is also written in I Peter 1:24,25 *"The voice said, Cry (cry out). And he said, what shall I cry? All flesh is grass, and all the goodliness (loveliness) thereof is as the flower of the field: The grass withereth, the flower fadeth: because the spirit (breath) of the LORD bloweth upon it: surely the people is grass. The grass withereth, the flower fadeth: but the Word of the God shall stand for ever."*

All people are equal in God's sight. It does not matter what position they sits in on this earth. It is true that many have excelled but you and I are as much a part of God's creation as they are. God is not a respecter of person. You may not be in the position that others are in, but yet you have within yourself what really counts with God – a heart of love, integrity, kindness, and compassion; these attributes give you status with God. Yes, these attributes are the real deal that gives you status when it comes down to comparison.

You can overcome the fear of man and the lack of self-confidence or insecurity that creates this fear. Say as the Psalmist said, *"In God I will praise His Word, in God I have put my trust; I will not fear what flesh can do unto me."* Psalm 56:4

Additional Scriptures reading dealing with lacking security and lacking confidence.

Deut. 31:1-8　　　　　　　　　　　Psalm 73:21-26
Psalm 108　　　　　　　　　　　　Philippians 4:10-20
I John 3:19-24

Fear No. 3
Rejection

rejection – 1. to be unwilling to accept, recognize, or make use of; 2. to refuse to grant;deny. 3. to throw out; discard.

We all desire to be accepted in some way, but there are times when we all have to deal with the negative feeling of rejection. The rejection of our work, the way we dress, race, culture, too tall, too fat, too short, the way we act, relationship, etc.

The Force:
An innate desire to please and be accepted.

When we are not acceptable to others or what represents us are not acceptable to others, – it hurts –, and the knife of rejection scars us.

Rejection says, "We are not a part, we do not belong and we are not loved." Our human thread says, "We need to belong." It's all right to have this need. We are designed to want to be loved, cared for, and belong.

If you desire to belong, make sure that which you are seeking to belong to is something good, honest, and pure.

Rejection tears through the fiber of our being. It wounds us to the point of depression, withdrawal from people, our potentials, and pursues. It causes us to deal with the dire feeling of unworthiness. It carries within itself: no value, no merit, no use and no worth. It's a poison to the human soul. Rejection has a voice that drives people to do what is not normal or right. Its results can be deadly – leading you to physically harm yourself or others.

Remember, the fear of rejection will hinder or stop your progress in life. It will rob you of your dreams.

Rejection is a hard and hurtful thing to cope with; but where there is an injury there is a healing balm. You can handle this negative fear successfully through the antidote below.

The Antidote:
1) You have to accept and live with these facts:
- **You are not perfect.**
- **You were not made to please everyone.**
- **You cannot please everyone, and**
- **You will not please everyone.**

2) An orderly relationship

We will experience rejection and its negative emotion we must be prepared to deal with it and overcome it when it occurs. We can also minimize the struggle of this negative emotion if we would line our relationships in the right order.

1) Be pleasing to the Lord.

"That ye might walk worthy of the Lord unto all pleasing, being fruitful in every good work, and increasing in the knowledge of God." Col. 1:10

2) Be pleasing to family (home).

"Wives, submit yourselves unto your own husbands, as it is fit(fitting) in the Lord. Husbands, love your wives, and be not bitter against them. Children, obey your parents in all things: for this is well pleasing unto the Lord. Fathers, provoke not your children to anger, lest they be discouraged." Colossians 3:18-21

Also see **Ephesians 6:1-4**

3) Be less pleasing to the world.

Servants, be obedient to them that are your masters according to the flesh, with fear and trembling, in singleness (sincerity) of your heart, as unto Christ; Not with eyeservice as men pleasers; but as the servants of Christ, doing the will of God from the heart; with good will doing service, as to the Lord, and not to men: Knowing that whatsoever good thing any man doeth, the same shall be receive of the Lord, whether he be bond(slave) or free." Eph. 6:5-8

Other verses on pleasing the Lord:

"But as we were allowed of God to be put in trust with the gospel, even so se speak; not as pleasing men, but God, which trieth our hearts." I Thess. 2:4

"Make you perfect in every good work to do his will, working in you that which is wellpleasing in his sight, through Jesus Christ; to whom be glory for ever and ever." Amen. Heb. 13:21

If you are struggling with rejection, get a handle on it. Deal with it now before it takes you prisoner. You can do this by prayerful reading, meditating, and confessing the Word of God.

Below is a list of Scriptures that will be of great benefit in overcoming this negative force.

Romans 8:31
Isaiah 52:13-53:12
Matthew 9:9-13
Luke 4:16-30
John 15:18-16:4
Ephesians 1:3-14
I Peter 2:1-10

Fear No. 4
Phobias (Unnatural Fears)

Because we are humans, we are faced with various kinds of fears. The first fear is ***common sense fear* that** is healthy and life saving. We declare, "I was afraid to jump of the mountain, I was afraid to beat the train, I was afraid to drink this or smoke that, or I was afraid to play with fire!" These actions – if carried out – will be life threatening, but because of common sense fear, so many of us are still alive.

Next, are ***natural fears.*** Natural fears can be define as: being afraid to do or carry out a certain task or action that is not life threatening or destructive; for example, being afraid to speak or perform before people. Natural fears are okay to experience, as long as, we have courage to get up and do it anyway. If natural fears wont let you go forward, then you are not necessarily in bondage you just lack courage. Pray for courage.

<u>courage</u> – *The quality of mind that enables one to face danger with confidence, resolution, and firm control of oneself; bravery.*

And the last on this list are ***phobias.*** Phobias are an intense, abnormal, or illogical fear of something.

The Force:
Demonic and non-demonic

demonic – an intense abnormal, or illogical fear that is invalid and can't be explained and has no root cause.

non-demonic – an intense, abnormal, logical fear that is valid and can be explained and has a root cause; such as, a tragic event that happened in one's life or a cruel punishment or tragic event that happened to another person in your presence.

The Antidote:
1) Receive Jesus into your heart
2) Pray
3) Put on the armour of God
4) Seek professional help

1) When you receive Jesus into your heart, you are born again and given power over fear – natural and demonic – in the world. *"For whatsoever is born of God overcometh the world: and this is the victory that overcometh the world, even our faith. Who is he that overcometh the world, but he that believeth that Jesus is the Son of God?"* I John 5:4,5

As a child of God, you are a new creature and are given power over fear (natural and demonic). *"Therefore if any man be in Christ, he is a new creature (creation): old things are passed away; behold, all things are become new."* II Corinthians 5:17

"For God hath not given us the spirit of fear; but of power, and of love, and of a sound mind." II Timothy 1:7

Fear is of the devil; Faith and authority is of God. Faith and authority is given to you to overcome the work of the enemy in the world. Whatever the source of these fears and phobias, you can reign victorious over them through the overcoming power of God, professional counseling, and therapy.

Behold I give unto you (authority) to tread (trample) on serpents and scorpions, and over all the power of the enemy: and nothing shall by any means hurt you." Luke 10:19

As a child of God, you receive a love that overcomes tormenting fear. God is love and God's Spirit dwells in you. And where the Spirit of the Lord dwells – there is liberty. ***"There is no fear in love; but perfect love casteth out fear: because fear hath (involves) torment. He that feareth is not made perfect in love."*** I John 4:18

"Now the Lord is that Spirit: and where the Spirit of the Lord is, there is liberty." 2 Corinthians 3:17

2) Pray for deliverance, strength and courage. If prayer along does not help, try fasting.

And he said unto them, " This kind can come forth by nothing, but by prayer and fasting." Mark 9:29

"Then shall ye call upon me, and ye shall go and pray unto me, and I will hearken (listen) unto you. And ye shall seek me, and find me when ye shall search for me with all your heart. And I will be found of you, saith the LORD: and I will turn away your captivity (bring you back from),…" Jeremiah 29:12-14

Have faith in God.
"Therefore I say unto you, What things soever ye desire, when ye pray, believe that ye receive them, and ye shall have them." Mark 11:24

Assurance of answered prayer.
"And whatsoever ye shall ask in my name, that will I do, that

the Father may be glorified in the Son. If ye shall ask any thing in my name, I will do it." John 14:13,14

3) Be dressed with the whole armour of God that ye may fight and stand victorious over these strongholds of fear.

"For though we walk in the flesh, we do not war after (according to) the flesh: For the weapons of our warfare are not carnal (of the flesh), but mighty through God to the pulling down of strong holds)" II Corinthians 10:3,4

"Finally, my brethren, be strong in the Lord, and in the power of his might. Put on the whole armour of God, that ye may be able to stand against the wiles (schemes) of the devil. For we wrestle not against flesh and blood, but against principalities, against powers, against the rulers of the darkness of this world (age), against spiritual wickedness in high places. Wherefore take unto you the whole armour of God, that ye may be able to withstand in the evil day, and having done all, to stand. Stand therefore, having your loins girt about with (gird your waist with) truth, and having on the breastplate of righteousness; And your feet shod with the preparation of the gospel; Above all, taking the shield of faith, wherewith ye shall be able to quench all the fiery darts of the wicked (wicked one). And take the helmet of salvation, and the sword of the Spirit, which is the Word of God:" Ephesians 6:10-17

If you want to take charge of your mind and life, you need to first take charge over fear. If you don't have what it takes, God will give it to you. He will give you courage to face the fears and bad memories. Bad memories have a way of afflicting a person for life. They disable and control your present and future. They affect your choices and decides your destiny. Bad memories are like black tar and quicksand.

You don't have to allow the blackness and the terror of bad memories to suffocate you. You can live! The event of that memory happened in the past. It is the memory that travels with us. We can't change the event or the memory of it, but we can change how it will affect our present and future.

Through power in Christ you can overcome.

"I can do all things through Christ which strengtheneth me."
Philippians 4:13

"Wait on the Lord: be of good courage, and he shall strengthen thine heart: wait, I say, on the Lord." Psalm 27:14

"Fear thou not: for I am with thee: be not dismayed; for I am thy God: I will strengthen thee; yea, I will help thee; yea, I will uphold thee with the right hand of my righteousness." Isaiah 41:10

Declaration: *"I shall not die, but live, and declare the works of the Lord."*
Psalm 118:17

4) Seek professional help.

Jesus said, *"They that be whole (are well) need not a physician, but they that are sick." Matt. 9:12*

Additional Scriptures for courage to face phobias (unnatural fears):

Deuteronomy 33:27   Philippians 4:6,8
Romans 8:38,39   Isaiah 51:11

Isaiah 43:2   Psalm 30:5
Psalm 31:24   I Peter 4:12,13
Isaiah 40:31

Remember that you can live a victorious life, if you believe. Jesus said unto him, *"If thou canst believe, all things are possible to him that believeth."* Mark 9:23 *and* *"With men it is impossible, but not with God: for with God all things are possible."* Mark 10:27

"If the Son therefore shall make you free, ye shall be free indeed." John 8:36

Barbara A. Perry is a Teacher of the Word of God and a Christian writer. She is the founder and senior pastor of Spirit of Prevailing Faith in Aiken, South Carolina. She has been a pastor for over 20 years. She is sole proprietor of Garden 33 Publisher. She is married to Jimmie Perry. 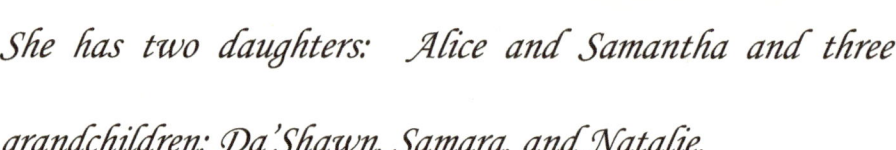 She has two daughters: Alice and Samantha and three grandchildren: Da'Shawn, Samara, and Natalie.

Other books by Barbara A. Perry:

The Blessing Of Numbers 6: 22 - 27

PIAS: Supernatural Sessions

Website: www.garden33publisher.com

Email: pastorbawp@yahoo.com

www.ingramcontent.com/pod-product-compliance
Lightning Source LLC
Chambersburg PA
CBHW031432040426
42444CB00006B/779